LOVE AND LOGIC PARENTING

Raising happy and well-behaved kids with positive thinking, love and responsibility

By
Harris brown

Table of contents

Introduction

Chapter 1: 15 Helpful Parenting Tips For Raising A Smart Kid
- **Frequently asked questions**

Chapter 2: How to Raise a confident child
- **Four Ways to Raise an Expressive Child**

Chapter 3: Be your child's lagend
- **Hints on how to be your child's legend**

Chapter 4: 10 techniques for making yourself your youngster's Legend

Conclusion

Introduction

The Love and Logic way to deal with nurturing is worked around the study of mindful and conscious connections. A credible, cherishing association among guardians and their kids frames the groundwork of appropriate conduct and solid direction.

Sounds adequately simple yet never before in history have guardians been confronted with such countless difficulties! Our methodology gives various straightforward and compelling procedures for nurturing kids from birth to adulthood. Whether you're setting out interestingly with your new child or exploring the violent adolescents with your kid, our procedures and methods will assist you with making quiet and adoring arrangements.

The "Rationale" in Love and Logic happens when we permit youngsters to simply decide, reasonable slip-ups and experience the normal or sensible outcomes. At the point when we offset this with true compassion, they foster the accompanying rationale: Our youngsters discover that the nature of their lives relies upon the nature of their decisions.

Chapter 1

15 Helpful Parenting Tips For Raising A Smart Kid

1. Center around the cycle as opposed to the outcome

A report distributed in Scientific American proposes that underlining the most common way of acquiring information and not on knowledge or capacity is vital to bringing up brilliant kids .

The investigation discovered that youngsters who are much of the time told by their folks and educators that they are savvy and keen deteriorated in their development contrasted with kids who created through consistent difficult work, assurance, and concentration.

Try not to applaud the youngster for the outcome. All things being equal, appreciate their work. It is basic you cause your kid to comprehend that achievement additionally incorporates conquering losses and troubles.

2. Peruse out loud to your kids

Frequently, guardians purchase costly toys and devices to ensure their youngsters advance rapidly while all they need is an exceptionally straightforward movement that can do ponder; perusing out loud. Research demonstrates that it assists kids with creating language and education abilities. Training requires only 15-20 minutes of your time, and you could begin it even before your kid begins going to class.

Likewise, when you read out loud, your kid will hear new words, in this manner working on their jargon.

3. Cause them to feel exhausted

It is difficult to keep ourselves connected with and engaged constantly. This is much more valid for youngsters. A flashing capacity to focus could add to the guardians' burdens. Fatigue, an expansive term that makes sense of the sensation of prompt lack of engagement in exercises, is many times thought about something negative. Nonetheless, weariness can do ponders and flash your kids' inventiveness

You shouldn't even need to be overloaded by keeping your kids connected consistently. Permit them to get exhausted, and really at that time they will figure out how to beneficially invest their energy.

4. Give a peaceful, solid climate

It is vital that a youngster has a solid sense of safety in their current circumstance. Stress of any sort can prompt weaknesses in learning and memory. Frequently, when guardians put a ton of weight on the youngster to perform better or when the connection between individuals at home isn't exceptionally encouraging, it can unfavorably influence the kid. The more joyful and more secure kids feel, the better they act and learn.

5. Be joined to your youngster

Studies have laid out a connection between the IQ scores of kids and how profoundly joined they are to their folks.

Research likewise demonstrates that nearby connection with guardians is basic to kids' close to home and social turn of events. Thus, it is essential that you stand by listening to your kid, visually connect, and regulate your manner of speaking, and so forth, to construct a safe connection with your kid.

6. Adjust your kid's ears to music

Music contacts the spirit and revives the brain. It likewise makes the mind more keen and more brilliant. A rising number of studies have demonstrated that music has an immediate association with how shrewd your youngster grows up to be. Music can affect the creating minds of small kids.

7. Give them a nutritious breakfast

A new report completed by the University of Pennsylvania School of Nursing has laid out an immediate connection between a normal, nutritious breakfast and higher IQ test scores in kids. The review noticed the nourishing and social parts of breakfast assume a crucial part in their verbal as well as scholastic exhibition.

The main dinner of the day, breakfast supplies indispensable minerals and nutrients to the cerebrum. Furthermore, social communication with relatives at the morning meal table permits youngsters to grow their jargon and general information and understand stories. Youngsters who eat day to day likewise have better memory and longer abilities to focus.

8. Energize unstructured play

Everyone figures out the significance of activity and recess in a kid's turn of events. It is even more critical that you guarantee your children practice their muscles and cerebrum and enjoy some unstructured recess. Free play helps in the improvement of interactive abilities and furthermore ignites imagination. It advances creative minds and sidelong reasoning.
This recess mustn't be restrictive to the games preparing that youngsters get in schools. Support deliberate play as it advances better learning and further develops language and critical thinking abilities.

9. Put kids to early sleep

Studies recommend that small kids need somewhere around 10 hours of rest every day. Youngsters with standard sleep times have been seen to have better memory, language abilities, and critical ability to think. Concentrates additionally recommend that we are bound to hold what we've realized whether we rest not long after our investigations.

10. Assist them with learning another dialect

Dialects assume a significant part in how your kids end up being. Youngsters have the intrinsic capacity to get dialects. Studies have likewise demonstrated that a youngster who learns a subsequent language or an unknown dialect before the age of ten is socially more educated and brilliant.

Kids get familiar with a language quicker, hold it better, and most frequently, talk it with an almost exact elocution than grown-ups. Ongoing exploration likewise shows that small kids can learn and deal with up to five dialects.

11. Guarantee a positive companion bunch for your kid

The sort of organization your youngster keeps in the area and at school will significantly affect them. In spite of the fact that we generally partner peer tension with adverse consequences, it can help youngsters and make them brilliant. A decent area, a fair school, and polite and curious youngsters around your kid will essentially affect your kid's learning. Presented to friends of different societies, they are probably going to ingest more data.

A concentrate by financial expert Bruce Sacerdote clarifies how strong this impact can be. He expresses that understudies with poor quality point midpoints showed an expansion in their scores when they cooperated and got to know higher scoring understudies.

12. Deal with their screen time

Concerns keep on being raised about the adverse consequences of delayed screen time in youngsters. Aside from youth weight and conduct issues, exorbitant screen time has additionally been connected to sporadic rest and absence of inventiveness. Furthermore, youngsters may likewise be presented to savage or sexual substance. Nonetheless, many guardians keep on contingent upon these computerized gadgets to engage their kids during their bustling timetables.

Troublesome as it could be to keep away from computerized association out and out, a little administration can help guardians. Permit age proper projects, and know about the commercials and how they impact kids' psyches. Likewise know about real screen time they get consistently. You could likewise urge your kid to learn different exercises that don't include screens.

13. Turn into their brilliant parent

Kids advance by copying their folks and elderly folks. In this manner, as guardians, you are their most memorable educators. Be brilliant to make them savvy. What you do is probably going to straightforwardly impact them. In the event that your kids see you perusing or composing, they are probably going to get a book and perused, and assuming they see you moving or singing, they will most certainly attempt to match your means. Essentially, drawn out screen use in guardians will likewise prompt expansion in youngsters' screen time.

Your way of behaving and activities significantly influence how your youngster creates propensities and gets a handle on the world. In this way, take part in imaginative talk and exercises that support their turn of events.

14. Include them in tasks

They may not do it entirely the initial time, however including kids in family tasks is advantageous for their turn of events and upgrades their mental, legitimate thinking, and the executives abilities. It relies heavily on how well you consolidate it in their daily practice.

These errands can be essentially as basic as arranging vegetables, tidying up the table, and collapsing garments. While at it, you can likewise show them estimations, computations, and using time productively and add an enjoyable to it.

15. Acquaint math with them from the get-go

Many guardians present math as a mind boggling subject to their kids, unwittingly imparting an apprehension about the subject in them. As indicated by research done by Dr. Greg Duncan, mastering math abilities from the get-go in life prompts later accomplishment and further developed consideration abilities.

The most effective way to do this is to present math in all things and mess around with numbers, whether it is including the devices in your home, arranging the great and terrible tomatoes, or skip counting the stairs

Often asked questions

1. What makes a kid smart?

Different factors like hereditary variables, natural elements, social impacts, financial status, and instructive open doors impact a kid's scholarly improvement capacities.

2. What are the indications of a savvy youngster?

A few indications of a brilliant kid incorporate superb memory, great interactive abilities, high IQ level, mature reasoning, Unique and imaginative considerations, and interest in perusing.

Guardians generally want their kids to be shrewd. Monitoring ways of bringing up a savvy youngster could assist with ingraining information and work with your kids' general development and improvement for the long run. Following specific viable tips like empowering perusing, unstructured recess, giving a calm climate, and a rich eating routine are critical to advancing your youngster's sound turn of events. Further, you might continue supporting and inspiring your kids to assist them with arriving at their maximum capacity and give your feedback and direction to try sincerely and accomplish their objective.

Chapter 2:
How to Raise a Confident Child

Confidence is your kid's identification to a long period of emotional wellness and social bliss. It's the groundwork of a youngster's prosperity and the way to progress as a grown-up. At all ages, what you feel about yourself means for how you act. Contemplate when you have a great outlook on yourself.

You presumably found it a lot more straightforward to coexist with others and inspirational about them. Attempt these tips and counsel to assist with bringing up a sure youngster.

The youngster searches in the mirror and likes the individual he sees.

He glimpses inside himself and is alright with the individual he sees.

He should consider himself being somebody who can get things going and who deserves love.

Guardians are the principal wellspring of a youngster's identity worth. Absence of a Good Self-Image Very Often Leads to Behavior Problems

A large portion of the social issues that I see for guiding come from unfortunate self-esteem in guardians as well as youngsters.

For what reason would one say one is an individual a joy to be with, while another consistently appears to drag you down?

How individuals esteem themselves, coexist with others, perform at school, accomplish at work, and relate in marriage all originate from the strength of their mental self view.

Solid Self-Worth Doesn't Mean Being Narcissistic or Arrogant

Assuming that you bring up a sure kid that grows up with solid self-esteem, it implies they have a reasonable comprehension of their assets and shortcomings, partaking in the qualities and figuring out the pain points.

Since there are such areas of strength between how your kid feels about himself and how he acts, it is essential to teach to bring up a certain youngster.

Over the course of life, your youngster will be presented with positive
impacts (manufacturers) and adverse impacts (breakers).

Guardians can open their kid to additional developers and assist him with managing the breakers.

Step by step instructions to bring up an expressive youngster but then conscious Bringing up a sincerely expressive youngster is one of the greatest difficulties of nurturing for those of us who weren't permitted to communicate our sentiments as kids. This is the way to urge your youngster to be expressive, yet aware.

Four Ways to Raise an Expressive Child

1. Practice Attachment Parenting

A child who can communicate needs turns into an express kid sentiments. For this reason we underline the significance of being receptive to your child's prompts.

A one-month-old cries to communicate his requirement for food or holding. Guardians get on these prompts and answer delicately. The child discovers that these driving forces inside himself have meaning. His cries bring ameliorating reactions.

Communicating his requirements prompts beneficial things. By being open and receptive to the child's prompts, guardians confirm the child's self-articulation.

At the point when guardians expect needs by perceiving inconspicuous pre-cry signals, the child learns a more noteworthy assortment of ways of communicating his thoughts and doesn't need to cry to get what he wants. This makes him a delight to have around, which guarantees that his folks will keep on being thoughtful to his requirements. The associated child turns into a fit kid of perceiving and showing profound sentiments.

Not so the detached newborn child. A child who is obediently planned, left to deal with it, and whose good natured guardians succumb to the anxiety toward ruining guidance, learns early that the providing care world isn't receptive to his requirements. He figures out how to quit inquiring. This child figures out how to disregard his sentiments at an early age. He learns neither to recognize nor to communicate with them. By all accounts, this little individual is a "great" child; he doesn't irritate anyone. He acclimates to the unyielding timetable, stays asleep from sundown to sunset, and is advantageous to have around. This "great" child, apparently so "very much focused," is in danger of turning into a removed youngster and an inside irate, discouraged grown-up. Other disengaged babies cry harder when they get no reaction, ending up being unpalatable and transparently irate. These infants become kids who are exceptionally difficult to make due. They convey these sentiments into adulthood, and like the "upside" child are in danger of winding up in the analyst's office. (This "great child" or "repulsive child" is unique in relation to the irritably simple child or troublesome child.)

2. Energize Toddler Feelings

The expressive child and responsive parent bring a triumphant blend into toddlerhood. Since the child's signs were paid attention to and decoded in the main year, the baby is better ready to communicate his thoughts. He is currently a greater individual with greater necessities. The baby who figured out how to communicate his necessities presently turns into the little child who is in contact with his sentiments. Moms tell us, "My baby doesn't have many words yet and it makes me attempt to figure him out." Martha has gotten extremely capable at perusing our little children's eyes. At the point when she doesn't know what the little child is "saying," she can get it together from the articulation in the eyes. The little child knows precisely the exact thing he is telling you, and his eyes frequently talk more smoothly than his tongue. Eagerly watching the eyes as your little child "opens up about his inner self" will frequently help the confused words unexpectedly check out.

3. Be Approachable

Babies are little people with huge necessities, who have a restricted capacity to impart these requirements. Help them. Meet your baby at eye-to-eye level when he is conversing with you. Be mindful in any event, when you don't have the foggiest idea what your little child is attempting to say. Give non-verbal communication signs (gesturing your head, eye-to-eye to eye connection, hand on shoulder) that you are attempting to grasp his perspective. In any event, when you can't stop what you are doing you can basically connect with your kid.

He isn't fully grown to comprehend the reason why your requirements are more pressing than his as of now, however hearing you converse with him ("Tell mother what you need... ") will assist him with feeling that you care about him.

Lauren, our kid, harms her finger. She holds her hurt finger dependent upon me, "Daddy, kiss owie." I know she's not exactly harmed, in light of the fact that she'd be crying in torment assuming she'd squeezed her finger hard. I could excuse this and return to my significant plan, yet my heart looks behind the eyes of my kid. I understand that this extremely solid looking finger isn't the issue. The way that Lauren feels her finger is harmed is the issue. Lauren learned she can utilize her sentiments to certainly stand out and my compassion, and by showing my own close to home interest in her situation, I can assist her with fostering her expressiveness and let her in on I care about her finger similarly as. "Show me where it harms. How gravely does it annoy you?" I investigate her eyes thoughtfully and delicately look at her finger. "Allow me to tell you the best way to improve it." I put a gauze on her finger or show her the best way to go to the cooler for the "blooper rabbit" (a fabric holder for ice blocks). I then hold her on my lap for a couple of moments until her consideration is redirected to a novel, new thing. The unpracticed parent might wonder whether or not to make such a fight over "nothing." The veteran acknowledges how delicate small kids are to unimportant injury to their bodies. From a kid's perspective, the smallest pinprick addresses an opening in his body, and he really wants the swathe to fix the break.

4. Abstain from Feeling-Stuffers

Youngsters can be irritating, depleting, and an out and out disturbance when they blow up to life's little misfortunes. Kids are that way. They appear to time their sensational exhibitions for the most badly designed time for their crowd. In any case, these "little" occasions mean quite a bit to them.

Try not to attempt to get a youngster to stuff her sentiments. At the point when a kid is disturbed, sit back, investigate her eyes, and give her existence to communicate her thoughts.

Fight the temptation to empty your response, outrage, judgment, rationale.

Your youngster isn't in an open outlook to get any of these.

Comments that convey your grown-up evaluation of the circumstance let the youngster know that she ought to stifle her own sentiments.

Feeling stuffers give the kid the message that you are not tolerating her feelings, and prompt the kid to hush. It's a dilemma.

The kid loses the capacity to articulate her thoughts, and you become an unaccepting guardian whose kid learns not to be open dependent upon you.

A distance is created between parent and kid.

Chapter 3
Be Your Child's Legend

Supporting the connection among father and youngster has forever been near my heart. All through my numerous long periods of private practice, I've spoken with many youngsters and adolescents - and something I love talking with them about is the relationship they have with their folks, and all the more explicitly, with their dad. A great deal of good and vices that I've found in children can be connected here and there to their collaborations with their father.

A ton of good and persistent vices in children can be connected here and there to their collaborations with their father.

Is father completely connected with steady areas of strength for and? Research shows, if so, the youngster or high schooler has a better profound, physical and otherworldly life. These children are less inclined to do crap rly in school, be engaged with unsafe ways of behaving as youths and young ladies particularly are less inclined to be physically dynamic from early on.

Is father far off, cool, grating or simply missing? These children are bound to grow up with an uneven close to home life and battle in the areas I recently recorded.

Presently I need to be honest and bring up that this isn't a dive in any capacity at single parents - you are astounding at bringing up your kid, and on the grounds that a dad isn't dynamic in your kid's life doesn't imply that they will battle here. While, doesn't eliminate the requirement for solid male impact in your youngster's life, which I discuss frequently. I'm letting you know this to make a vital point: kids need their dads.

All the more critically, youngsters need their dads. Kids see you, their dad, as their Legend. Allow me to put it another way:
Would you like to know more about your children? They aren't anticipating flawlessness. Kids are loaded with beauty for their folks, and

regardless of whether you commit an error; assuming you apologize and say you were off-base - they will in any case hold you in that extraordinary spot in their souls. They will in any case consider you to be their definitive legend.

Father, regardless of whether you know it, you are the focal point of your children's reality. So how would you maintain that title, father? In the event that you're stressed over wrecking it, that lets me know that you are as of now profoundly put resources into making an enduring, positive relationship with your kid. This is Uplifting news.

Hints on how to be your child's lagend

1. Be there.

That is all there is to it. Truly. Nothing establishes a greater amount of a connection with youngsters than when their dad appears and is purposeful in investing energy with them. Simply showing your child or girl that you need to invest energy with them will establish a long term connection.

Supportive Tip: These particular times enjoyed with your children ought not be tied in with streamlining things, talking through issues or contending. These times ought to be tomfoolery, light and charming. Show your children that you love being with them. Furthermore, don't fall into the snare of giving your children everything except YOU. Ordinary, decide to provide your youngsters with the endowment of presence.

2. Lead, don't mentor.

What's the distinction, you inquire? Where mentors essentially show abilities and empower their execution, chiefs are intended to bring vision and moral initiative. Your guidance and model are the compasses for your youngster as they grow up. Assuming that you tell them the best way to adore well, regard others, endure in difficult situations and adhere to reality come what may, you are placing your kid in a good position throughout

everyday life. Experience every day recalling that your kid is watching your decisions and responses. Be the pioneer they trust you to be. Fathers, be energized. It is NEVER past time to fire your children. Whether you are spic and span at this father business or you're quite a while in, you can continuously execute change and improvement in your associations with your children. They have loved you since the very beginning and they trust in you significantly more than you put stock in yourself.

Chapter 4
10 techniques for making yourself your youngster's Legend

1. Be their security.

Each kid needs to have a good sense of reassurance. As their father, they shift focus over to you to give that inclination consistently. At the point when those little eyes gaze toward you, they see Superman. Satisfy everyone's expectations.

2. Open your heart.

In the public eye, men are supposed to be areas of strength. This is something worth being thankful for. Nonetheless, with your kids, open all of yourself to them. Show them empathy, compassion, and absolution. They will, thus, do likewise with their children when they grow up.

3. Love and regard your significant other or their mom.

Your kids will figure out how men ought to act from you. Treat your better half or the youngster's mom with delicate consideration and the highest regard. On the off chance that you are hitched you can't cherish your better half impeccably, yet your children ought to never question your adoration for her. In the event that your youngsters are brought up in a caring marriage, they have an extraordinary model for future connections.

4. Peruse them.

Small kids like just to pursue a story. It illuminates their minds and gives them time with you. They likewise love it when you make it a stride further and add audio cues and entertaining voices. There could be no better solid than the unadulterated chuckling of your own kids.

5. Grasping your youngsters.

Regardless of how like you he might be, your kid has his own special character. Find an opportunity to get familiar with your kid and grasp him. What really matters to him? What makes him miserable? What is his fantasy? Kids need your affirmation of what their identity is.

6. Be friendly.

The gleam on a youngster's face when his father gets him with solid arms is a wonderful sight to see. Never be embarrassed to embrace your kid, kiss your kid, and say, "I love you". This comes hard for certain men, yet it very well may be the distinction between your youngster feeling adored or disliked.

7. Show your children.

Show your children the fundamental abilities they need. At times guardians relegate undertakings and simply expect a youngster knows how to do them. At the point when things spring up that you are not perfect at, learn them together. Be modest and clear and give your children all they should find actual success.

8. Dine with them.

It is a bustling world we live in. Supper time gets dissipated, covered, and covered without any problem. At the point when at all conceivable, ensure your family takes a seat at one table and offers feasts together - TV off. You won't ever more deeply study your kid in some other setting than at a supper table.

9. Tell them the best way to live.

One of the greatest nurturing botches is losing yourself simultaneously. Allow your kids to see everything that makes you magnificent. The family starts things out, yet the things you are energetic about don't need to bite the dust since you're a parent. At the point when your children see their father carrying on with a full and great life, they will in all likelihood do the equivalent when they are grown-ups.

10. Acquire new abilities.

"The day you quit learning new things is the day you start gradually kicking the bucket. "The day you quit learning new things is the day you start gradually passing on. Regardless of how old you get, learn constantly. Times change, new innovation is created, and we really want to adjust to it. Figure out how to fix things around the house and in the engine. Take care of a business who can stand his ground in a kitchen. This is a confusing world and your kids will take on your flexibility.

Conclusion

Nurturing is vital. Powerful nurturing assumes a crucial part regardless of whether a youngster turns into a useful citizen. At the point when kids get the legitimate love and backing, it helps the youngster grow appropriately and assists them with having the right mentality about existence and its challenges.Proper nurturing tells the kid what's in store out of life and how to manage them also. No parent ought to maintain that their kid should need to shift focus over to any other person other than for direction and support.Parenting styles doesn't necessarily need to be severe.

However long the parent is steady with the principles given I accept youngsters will follow them more with any issues.

At the point when guardians attempt to be requesting that is the point at which the kid essentially disses and winds up having problematic ways of behaving.

Providing the youngster with some sort of trust permits the kid to turn out to be more dependable and to be more developed.

Permitting the kid independence is significant also.

It is imperative that the parent is dynamic in their youngster's dating life as well as the parent actually must converse with their kid about anything.If the parent is steady with offering the kid directions and guidance then the kid will possibly go to the parent first for help and direction.

Age doesn't make any difference; nurturing ought to constantly be a piece of a parent's plan. Great correspondence, directing the utilization of rules reliably, and support is what a kid needs consistently.

Printed in Great Britain
by Amazon